In A Greer County Kitchen

A culinary memoir

Elaine DiRico

&

David Brookins

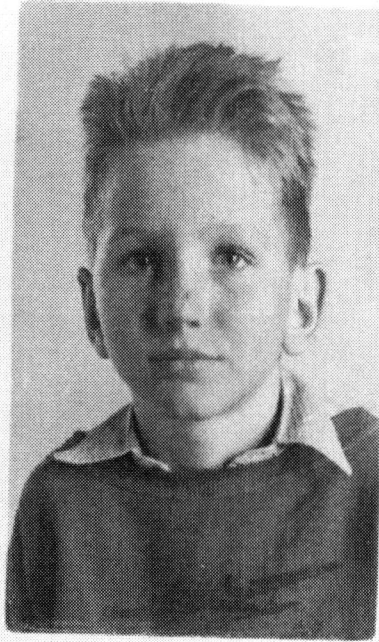

SCHOOL DAYS 1943-'44
Granite School

For Uncle Pete

Grocery on West side of Main St. Granite, Oklahoma, 1938

Introduction

In early June of this year my family gathered in Granite Oklahoma to celebrate the life of my Aunt Billie. She was married to the baby in my Mother's family, my Uncle Pete, and had passed away quietly at 91 years old. My sister flew from Scotland, where she now lives, I drove with her from Austin, and my cousins Steven and Kent came from Austin also. David lives in Blanchard Oklahoma, and has always had a deep connection to the ranch in Granite. His interest in the photographs and documents has lasted several decades and were an amazing window into the times I wanted to write about. We realized that it was the first time we were all gathered in twenty five years. Memories, and ideas and ways of life were slipping away, and especially recipes and food stories; my obsession. This little book is the result.

Uncle Pete, an absolute prince among men, scoured the kitchen and cookbooks, and I pulled the boxes with my mother's papers out and started sorting. One thing became clear quickly. What looked like recipes were in fact notes, missing specifics, and even ingredients on occasion. For an experienced, cook, this can work, especially if she was the one who made the notes. The second thing was availability of ingredients and changes in food preferences. Ultimately, what you find here are recreations, most of which I have tested, that are evocative of what we ate when we visited the ranch.

This has been such a wonderful time for me. Like most families, memories around food are happy and a kitchen is my Happy Place. Many things I had forgotten became vivid, like picking strawberries, and being scolded for eating so many, denying it despite a face covered in red juice. I remember picking peaches so ripe that the fruit came off in my hand, leaving the stem and seed on the tree. One summer we picked and canned a mountain of black eyed peas and since then the dried and soaked ones still taste like sawdust to me. A spa treatment has nothing on canning tomatoes in July in Oklahoma, with an aerobic workout, steam bath and often face and hand peel from the steam. But oh my, how lovely those red jars of sunshine are in January.

So here it is. I wanted to create a window to a time that we tend to romanticize, but which was in fact, grueling. When Mama and Papa Tittle got to Greer County, their house was built of logs, water was carried or hand pumped, and heat was from hand chopped and hauled wood. The focus of everyone was food- growing harvesting, cooking and preserving, at the whim of drought and ice and tornadoes. They were tough and courageous and I am proud to have their blood in my veins.

Jennie Tittle Stimson

Milton Alexander Stimson

Sam Houston Tittle

Spring

"We know we belong to the land,

And the land we belong to is grand!"

Greer county Oklahoma is predominantly rural, and every spring begins a new farming cycle. Pre-Internet, much of the 'seed surfing' was done at the feed store and through seed catalogues. Burpee's has been around since the late 1800's and contrary to the common story, was not named after the introduction of the first 'burpless' cucumber seed, but rather after the founder, W. Atlee Burpee. His son, David Burpee took over in 1915, and with the introduction of the mail order catalogue and Victory Gardens, became the leading seed distributor for vegetable gardens. Just as I love paging through and imagining a bountiful harvest, I can imagine my ancestors poring over the illustrations and promises of heavy red tomatoes and early onions. Sans television and internet, I am sure this was great entertainment, and prompted much discussion around dinner tables, as the weather warmed and the last of the home canned food was eaten.

Spring also brings wildflowers, Indian paintbrush, Scottish thistles, some north blown seeds of Texas bluebonnets and sunflowers. Many of the early settlers planted flower gardens, especially roses. The hearty progeny of these can still be seen in cemeteries and around abandoned farm houses, having adapted to a sometimes harsh climate. On the fence out the west facing kitchen window, Grandmother always had a well established heavenly blue morning glory thriving, surely the best named flower. It came back every year from 'volunteers'.

Spring planting also brought longer days, more work, and often added farmhands to the table. Hearty fare was called for, and the first lettuces and radishes were more garnish than anything. My Aunt Frances had a recipe for 'Shoe Peg Salad' that would work well.

Shoe Peg Salad

1 can shoe peg corn

1 can Le Sueur green peas

1 can green beans

1 (4 oz) jar diced pimentos

½ cup chopped scallions

1 minced green pepper (and jalapeno, optional)

1/2 teaspoon salt

1 teaspoon ground pepper

1/3 cup cider vinegar

½ cup good oil (olive)

¼ cup honey

Drain the canned vegetables, then mix them in a large bowl with the onions, and green peppers. Put the other ingredients in a jar and shake well to blend. Pour over the vegetables and mix, then keep in the refrigerator for 24 hours before serving, stirring occasionally.

A cold plate of that and ice tea would sound wonderful after a few hours in the field. Another cold salad I remember from Grandmother's refrigerator was:

Ham and Pea salad
1 cube cubed ham

1 cup cubed Velveeta

1 can Le Sueur peas, drained

½ cup chopped green onions

¾ cup Miracle Whip

Salt and pepper to taste

Stir all ingredients together and refrigerate 2-3 hours before serving. A variation of this replaces the Miracle Whip with Ranch Dressing. After refrigerating, stir in a pound of cooked macaroni. Oklahoma pasta salad, suitable for pot lucks, funerals and church functions. I decided once to make this using fresh peas. While it was okay, it didn't stir up my memory cravings like this did.

Pimento cheese is another classic, and I hate to imagine how much of it I have eaten over the years. A friend puts it into her mashed potatoes, to good effect. While I have always thought of pimento cheese as a quintessentially Southern recipe, it was actually started in New York.

Around 1885, Spain began sending their jarred red peppers to the United States, where their bright color and inoffensive flavor made them hugely popular. The original recipe was developed to combine them with cream cheese, another new and inoffensively flavored product. As home-ec teachers spread the word and the recipe moved south, it, like all good stories and recipes, began to evolve and develop some character. I remember Grandmother's being mild, but that may have been because she was often preparing it for kids. In 1907, Eva Green Fuller's *Up to Date Sandwich Book* suggested grinding 'two jars of Spanish pimentos with two cakes of Neufchatel cheese, season with a little salt and spread on thin slices of lightly buttered white bread.' In 2003, Southern Foodways Alliance in Oxford, Mississippi hosted a Pimento Cheese Invitational, drawing over 300 entrants. And while this Yankee interloper is considered to be more Southern than Oklahoman, it is definitely in my memory bank from Greer County.

Pimento Cheese

1 pound cheddar cheese, grated

1 cup mayonnaise, or Miracle Whip, if you are of that faction

1 -7 ounce jar pimentos, chopped

Mix together and store, covered, in a jar in the refrigerator for up to a week, although mine has never lasted that long. Add to your mashed potatoes like my friend Jack, to grits, or heat in a baking dish for an improvised queso. And customize the flavor with your own additions:

Chopped onions, or onion powder, or a pinch of garlic powder. Hot sauce is de riguer in our household, and a little chopped jalapeno, especially if you can find a couple of ripe red ones. The winner of the Pimento Cheese Invitational added a little sugar which boggles my mind, but okay.

Austin Furniture, Granite, Oklahoma, Jan. 31, 1948
(taken with a Brownie camera)

My mother sometimes made a carrot dish that she called 'Copper Pennies.' I found the recipe, in her handwriting in the one cookbook I inherited from her, 'The Good Housekeeping Cookbook.' I believe it was a wedding gift from my Grandmother Jenny, the 1942 edition. There is a 30 page addition printed on blue paper in the middle, titled 'Wartime Suggestions.' It was the first cookbook I remember using, a tan rust and orange plaid fabric cover. Here is her recipe, followed by an adaptation of my own. Fresh spring carrots are hard to beat!

Copper Pennies

2 pounds carrots sliced in rounds

½ cup sugar

¼ cup salad oil

¾ cup white vinegar

1 bunch scallions, chopped

1 Tablespoon French's mustard

2 teaspoons Worscestershire sauce

1 can condensed tomato soup

Cook the carrot slices in boiling salted water until just tender. Mix the remaining ingredients and por over the carrots. Refrigerate overnight. (I remember a turquoise glass bowl with a white milk glass interior and how pretty these looked in it.)

Jamaican Carrots

1 pound carrots sliced in rounds

2 Tablespoons olive oil or butter

1 12 ounce bottle good quality ginger beer

1 bunch scallions, chopped

Salt and pepper

Chopped jalapeno (optional)

In a wide saucepan, heat the oil or butter over medium high heat, add the carrots and toss to coat well. Drop the heat to low, add the ginger beer. Let cook until the carrots are tender and the liquid is reduced to a glaze. Salt and pepper to taste and serve hot, cold or room temperature, topped with the scallions and optional jalapeno.

Of course, deviled eggs are another classic, and with more sun, the hens will start laying again. These are an easy and efficient (and cheap) way to get needed protein into workers putting in long hours.

Improvisation and recycling were necessary skills.

Deviled Eggs

A dozen hard boiled eggs split lengthwise

2 Tablespoons mayonnaise*

1 Tablespoon sweet pickle relish

Paprika for garnish

Separate the yolks from the whites, laying the whites, hollow side up on a serving plate. (If an egg white gets too damaged to fill, incorporate it into the yolk mixture) Mash the yolks, and pickle relish together, spoon into the eggs and sprinkle with paprika.

*I contacted my fellow cooks with questions and asking for recipes, and it appears that, at least in the past, there was a rather strongly felt feud between the mayonnaise contingent (western Oklahoma and Texas) and the Miracle Whip folks, largely northeastern and central) until you got southeast, where Duke's mayonnaise had a following. Miracle Whip was developed by Kraft Foods in 1933, looking f or a cheaper alternative to mayonnaise, and gained favor with families wanting to lower their fat intake in the fifties. It was labeled: 'salad dressing spread' as the lowered fat content kept it from qualifying as mayonnaise. However the raised sugar volume kept the calories about the same. Duke's, created by Mrs. Eugenia Duke in 1917 has more eggs and zero sugar, and a lot of fans, including me. As with all cooking, follow your own palate.

Deviled eggs are a good canvas for just about anything, from chopped fresh herbs to better to caviar. One of my favorites had a good wallop of horseradish and chopped chives.

String Bean Salad

1 ½ pounds trimmed string beans

1 Tablespoon salt*

½ cup chopped white onions

2 Tablespoons salad oil**

1 teaspoon sugar

¼ cup vinegar

¼ cup water

4 ounce jar chopped pimentos, drained

Salad greens

Cook the string beans in boiling water with the Tablespoon of salt until tender-crisp, about 20 minutes. Put remaining ingredients, except the salad greens into a jar and shake vigorously to mix well. Pour over the beans, and chill for several hours, then serve on a bed of salad greens.

- This looks like a huge amount of salt in these 'enlightened' times, but most does go down the drain, and it is the only seasoning the beans will get.

- Vegetable oil is generic for just about any oil you want to use, so use a good quality and flavorful one like olive oil.

The marinated salad is a great genre and works well with any vegetable, raw or cooked. Changing up the ingredients can give instant variety and make seasonal cooking easy. Adding in a can or two of beans helps stretch the ingredients and adds fiber and nutrition.

Bean Salad

3 cans of beans, all different*

1 chopped red onion

1 chopped bell pepper

½ cup olive oil

¼ cup red wine vinegar

Salt and pepper to taste

Drain the beans and rinse well, then toss with the remaining ingredients. Chill for several hours before serving. Adding chopped fresh herbs like parsley brightens the flavor.

*Mother used red kidneys, yellow wax beans and garbanzos and often took this to pot luck picnics.

Marinated salads are a fine way to stretch vegetables, make them more appealing and since they need to chill and marinate, could be made the night before, important when you need everyone in the fields and garden before the heat of the day. They are also more satisfying then a green salad, especially with the addition of beans. Here is a salad I make ahead when it is too hot to cook, that we can snack on as we like. It is fine over greens for a meal, and good as an appetizer. It gets better the next day, but I haven't had it last longer than that.

Don's Antipasto Salad

½ pound good salami, sliced in bites

½ pound pitted olives

1 jar pepperoncini peppers, sliced

1 small red onion, minced

3 stalks celery, chopped

1 pound cherry tomatoes, halved

Handful of cauliflower florets, chopped

½ pound provolone, chopped to bite size

1 bunch flat leaf parsley, chopped

½ cup good olive oil

Juice of a lemon plus zested peel

Freshly ground black pepper

As with the other salads, toss everything together and chill well. By the time the salad is finished, there is a lot of liquid in the bottom of the bowl which makes a nice salad dressing.

One of the very best dishes I remember from Grandmother's table was her green beans cooked with pork and new potatoes. This is as close as I can come to hers, after several tries. There was a smoke house on the farm in Granite, but by the time my folks bought the ranch it was used for storage. . I well remember Granddad chasing an escaped hog down the creek, and my mother trying to cover four ears so my sister and I wouldn't hear what he was shouting. Ham and bacon were precious commodities, used as a seasoning more often than a meal. I still have the cast iron pot, that probably held fifteen gallons of water, that was used when they butchered, made soap, and I imagine did laundry. By the time we came along, there was a washateria in town with the wringer type washers. One of my earliest memories is my braid getting caught in the wringer when I was barely tall enough to see in the tub.

Green Beans and New Potatoes
2 pounds green beans, cleaned and trimmed

¼ pound salt pork or bacon, chopped

2 Tablespoons bacon fat

2-3 cloves garlic, minced

1 ½ cups stock (ham or chicken)

2 pounds new potatoes (golf ball sized)

1 thinly sliced yellow onion

Salt and pepper

2 Tablespoons butter

Brown the pork in the bacon fat, then add the green beans. Toss well and cover, then add the stock, cooking over medium low until they soften, about 15 minutes. Add the potatoes (some cooks peel a strip off each potato which may make it absorb more flavor) Cover again, and cook fifteen minutes more until the potatoes are softening, then add the onions and garlic, cover and cook another ten minutes until they are soft. Season to taste with salt and pepper, toss with the butter and serve.

Milton Stimson with 1915 Harley Davidson

Chapter two: Funeral Food

'Poor Judd is dead, poor Judd Fry is dead.

All gather round his coffin now and cry.

He wasn't very old, and he had a heart of gold,

Oh why did such a feller have to die?'

Funerals are important in small towns, and Greer county Oklahoma has nothing but small towns. Naturally, the older I get the more funerals I have been to, including my Aunt Billie's in June which precipitated this book. Billie was married to my mother's baby brother, Isaac Houston Stimson, aka Pete and on occasion I.H. The family lore says that my Granddaddy Stimson called an orphan calf Pete and the name stuck.

When Pete got out of the military in the mid 50s, he traded his small Harley Davidson for a 1948 Harley Davidson flathead ostensibly to herd cattle. I remember being perhaps 5 years old, which would make my uncle about twenty three. He put my twin sister and me in front of him on the Harley and took off towards town, and although my mother has been gone for twenty five years, I can still hear her screaming after us: "Isaac Houston Stimson, you bring those girls back here this second!!" We were going perhaps 20 mph, and it was the thrill of our lives.

Milton Stimson with Steven and David Brookins 1955

I digress. Billie's was a wonderful funeral. Billie was well known and well loved in the church. After a lot of nearly anonymous eulogies over the last few years, it was emotional and lovely to hear one delivered by someone who not only knew Billie well but had loved her. And after the service of course, there was lunch.

Funeral food is different from everyday food, and different across the country. In the middle of farm country, with grocery stores some distance away, food for the grieving family was made from what you had in the pantry and later the freezer. Casseroles and 'congealed salads' and desserts reigned. This first recipe is one I remembered Mother making.

Chicken Divan

2 10 ounce packages frozen broccoli

4 cups cooked chicken coarsely chopped

1 cup mayonnaise

2 cans cream of chicken soup

1 ½ teaspoon curry powder

½ pound Velveeta sliced

1 cup bread crumbs

3 Tablespoons butter

Cook the broccoli for three minutes in boiling water, drain well, and spread in the bottom of a well oiled 9"x13" baking pan. Spread the chicken on top of the broccoli. Mix together the soup, mayonnaise and curry powder and pour over the chicken mixture. Place the sliced Velveeta across the top. Brown the bread crumbs in the butter. Top the casserole with the crumbs, and back for 30-40 minutes in a 350 degree oven.

If you have had a garden, you know what it is like when the summer squash start coming in. At a funeral, food will be served buffet style, so a squash dish is iffy to balance on a paper plate. Here is a solution.

Summer Squash Squares

3 cups grated summer squash

1 cup Bisquick

½ cup chopped onions

½ cup grated Parmesan

1 package frozen chopped spinach

½ teaspoon each dried marjoram, oregano and garlic

Salt and pepper

½ cup oil or butter or bacon drippings

4 beaten eggs

Liberally oil a 9"x13" ovenproof casserole dish. Place all the ingredients in a large bowl and mix well, then spread in the casserole and bake for 30-40 minutes at 350 degrees. Let cool then cut into squares to serve.

And though it is Texan, I imagine that an occasional King Ranch Casserole shows up at a funeral dinner.

King Ranch Casserole

I can each cream of mushroom and cream of chicken soup

1 cup chicken broth

1 can Ro-tel tomatoes

2 cloves garlic, chopped

1 can black olive slices

1 can chopped green chilies

12 8" corn tortillas cut in quarters

Meat from a 3-4 pound roast chicken, chopped

1 chopped yellow onion

1 chopped bell pepper

2 cups grated 'Mexican Blend' cheese (cheddar and Jack)

Oil a 9"x13" ovenproof casserole dish. Preheat oven to 350 degrees. In a large saucepan, heat the soup, broth, tomatoes, garlic, olives and chilies until warm, remove from the heat. Layer the casserole dish with half the tortillas, then a layer of chicken, sprinkled with half of the onion and bell pepper, topped with the cheese. Repeat the layers, starting with tortillas and ending with cheese. Bake for 30-40 minutes until bubbling and the cheese beginning to brown.

Pretty much a classic formula: 2-3 cups of protein, 3 cups starch, a gravy of sorts, usually in the form of canned condensed soup, seasoning. Spread in an oiled casserole dish (9"x13") and bake for 30 minutes or until GBD, Golden Brown and Delicious. That combination has yielded some amazing family recipes. But its true beauty shines when you are miles from a grocery store, with a lot of hungry people and a meager pantry. Because I am used to a car, a nearby store, a refrigerator and freezer, I can romanticize living on the ranch in the early 20th century, but the facts are much less comfortable. Grueling days, dust storms, floods, and drought made life a lot less comfortable. I asked Pete what kind of wood they cut for the cook stove last night: 'Anything that would burn!' I went and kissed my gas stove, hugged my refrigerator and dishwasher.

Fried chicken is another classic at funerals and my mother's specialty. When we visited Granite, the three siblings, Mother, Aunt Frances and Pete were often there along with my cousins. An astounding amount of food passed through the kitchen then, and an even more astounding pile of dishes got hand washed in a sink a little larger than the sink in my bathroom. I know, because I spent a lot of time standing on a chair to wash them. (Just went to kiss my huge double sink and pat the dishwasher again.) But with Grandmother, the sisters and me in the kitchen, it felt less like work than usual.

Here is how Mother fried chicken. I remember Grandmother using bacon drippings and later Crisco for frying, and Mother used vegetable oil. Follow your heart and taste buds. Cast iron is the standard for cooking. I have one that was Grandmother's and Mother's and it is used more than anything else in my kitchen. And always fry more than you will need, because people will eat more than you think and there is nothing as good as cold fried chicken.

Bobbie Jean's Fried Chicken

2 chickens cut into 8 pieces*

2 cups all purpose flour in a brown paper bag

1 Tablespoon garlic salt

1 Tablespoon ground black pepper

Fat for frying

Add the garlic salt and pepper to the flour in the bag and shake to mix. Put your cast iron skillet on the stove on medium high heat, and add enough fat to come up ½" deep. As it heats, have a plate by the stove for the breaded chicken pieces. Place the pieces, 2 at a time, in the bag with the flour, shake to coat and move to the plate. When the fat is 325 degrees (a sprinkle of flour tossed in bubbles immediately) add the pieces, skin side down, laying them down away from you to avoid getting splattered. Do Not Crowd The Skillet!! This is fried chicken, not steamed chicken. Watch carefully, and when the skin side is a deep golden brown, use tongs to turn the pieces. Drop the heat to medium low, cover and let cook for 20 minutes or until the second side is well browned and the juices run clear. If you use a meat thermometer, you want the breast meat to be 160 degrees. Drain on a rack over newspaper or paper towels.

- Cut the chicken by quartering it, separating the leg from the thigh, then splitting the breast in half, cutting away from the bone if you like, and cutting each breast half in half again. This gives you roughly equal sized pieces so that it can cook evenly.

- There is controversy about rinsing chickens. Commercially raised chickens, often have salmonella. My feeling is that rinsing can spread the germs, so I do not, but I am careful to contain the area and clean it well with hot soapy water and a vinegar rinse.

Just as with Mother's carrot recipe, I have tweaked this one a bit. I cut up my chicken and brine it in buttermilk and hot sauce with a ½ teaspoon of baking soda. I find it crisper and more juicy and tender. I drain it a bit and let it dry some before tossing with the flour.

Up next- congealed salads, also rather formulaic. Jello has been around since 1904. It used to be a long process of boiling bones down, straining, defatting and then flavoring the stuff, and was saved for the wealthy and the sick. It is still good food, but once dyed, flavored and sweetened, (88% sugar?) the health benefits may be questionable. But as a binder for various ingredients, it is perfect.

Green Jello Salad

1 can crushed pineapple

1 cup chopped celery

12-15 marshmallows (optional)

1 package lime Jello

½ cup chopped pecans

1 cup cottage cheese

1 cup whipped topping

Drain the pineapple juice into a measuring cup, adding enough water to make 1 ½ cups. Pour into a saucepan and bring to a boil (if you are using marshmallows, add them now to melt.) Add the lime Jello and stir to dissolve. Remove from the heat and let cool for 15 minutes or until thickened. Add the pineapple, cottage cheese, nuts and whipped topping, stir to blend, pour into a mold and chill until set

That one is a classic, and delicious. I suspect, without the marshmallows and less sugar, it would pass for a health food now. As I said, pretty formulaic. Change up the flavor of jello, and the fruit, and you have a different salad.

Always at funerals, there are several potato dishes. What could be more comforting than potaotes, especially drowned in something rich? A friend sent me this recipe for 'Funeral Potatoes' and it struck a memory of a dish someone brought to my Mother's funeral. I may not be good at remembering names, but I am very good at remembering food, even decades later.

Funeral Potatoes

1 two pound bag of shredded hash brown potatoes

2 cups sour cream

2 cups shredded sharp cheddar plus ½ cup for topping

2 cans cream of chicken soup

½ cup bacon crumbles (optional)

½ cup chopped scallions

2 cups Corn flakes lightly crushed

Preheat oven to 350 degrees. In a large bowl, mix the sour cream, soup and cheese. Add the potatoes and stir well to mix. Turn into a well oiled 9"x13" baking dish, and bake for 35-40 minutes. Mix the corn flakes, bacon and remaining half cup of cheese, and top the casserole, return to the oven for 15 minutes. Serve hot or room temperature.

As the characters in 'Oklahoma' found there is no place hotter for a funeral than Oklahoma when you're running out of ice. While this recipe, also from a friend breaks the funeral food credo of freezing well, it is wonderful in the heat, served very cold, and leftovers are rarely a problem. It was written in my mom's handwriting, but I don't believe I ever tasted it until I tried the recipe.

Cold Macaroni Salad

1 pound elbow macaroni, cooked according to directions and drained

1 bottle ranch salad dressing

2 packages frozen peas and carrots

1 bunch green onions, chopped

Toss everything in a pretty bowl, and chill well. Serve in a smaller bowl that can be replenished to make sure it stays cold.

I remember a story about a woman in a small town who reputedly fried a chicken every morning so that if someone died, she would be the first one to the family's house to find out what happened. If you boiled the macaroni, tossed it with a little olive oil so it wouldn't stick together, and froze it, this salad could come together out of the pantry in under a minute, and already be chilled. You could beat fried chicken lady to the house.

Pies and cakes and cobblers and sweets are the best comfort food, and good for funerals, but that is another whole chapter.

Any heavily agricultural area has a demographic of migrant workers, most often from Mexico. Luckily for all of us, this has contributed to the cuisine in Greer County. One of my favorite dishes, and one that often goes to potlucks is tamale pie. This recipe serves a LOT of people.

Tamale Pie
serves a crowd

2 boxes Jiffy corn muffin mix

2 eggs

1 cup buttermilk

1 cup creamed corn

1 cup 1 c chopped onion

2 Tablespoons oil

2 1/2 teaspoons ground cumin

1 cup enchilada sauce (1 can Old El Paso)

1 Tablespoon minced garlic

1 Tablespoon chili powder

2 pounds ground beef

1-2 cans chopped green chilies (optional)

3 cups shredded cheese (Monterrey jack, Cheddar or a mix)

salt and pepper

chopped cilantro and jalapenos for garnish

Preheat your oven to 400 degrees. In a large, heavy skillet, saute onions In the oil until they are just beginning to brown. Add the cumin and chili powder, stir to combine, then add the garlic and cook for one minute over medium heat. Break up the meat and add to the skillet, and cook, stirring, until well browned. add the chilies if you like. Taste and add salt and pepper as needed. set aside to cool.

In a large bowl combine the corn muffin mix, buttermilk, creamed corn and egg, whisk until evenly combined. Pour into a large, deep cast iron skillet and bake for 20 minutes, until brown. Let cool for five minutes, then with a fork, puncture the surface of the cornbread well and saturate with the enchilada sauce. Top with the meat, spread evenly, then the cheese. Cover with foil and return to the oven for 20 minutes, then remove the foil and broil until the cheese browns, about five minutes.

Mama Tittle holding Jennie, Louis and Papa Tittle 1905

Chapter 3: Sweets

'I'm just a girl who cain't say no. I'm in a terrible fix!

I always say 'Come on, let's go,' just when I ought to say nix.'

Looking through the old recipes, I was astounded by the number of desserts! But as I went through pictures and cookbooks and got a better image of life in Greer County at the beginning of the twentieth century, it made sense. Often the days were sunrise to sunset and longer, hard manual labor, often repetitive. There was a need to get a lot of calories into folks fast and efficiently. Sugar and flour kept well and often milk and eggs were gathered daily and needed to be used. How things have changed. The next time I am feeling nostalgic for the farm meals I remember (or have fanaticized) I just need to remind myself that if I want to be working hard, lifting bales of hay into wagons drawn by mules, stacking the hay in the barn, feeding the livestock, and cooking for a lot of family and farmhands, then finally sitting down... with the mending, I too can have four or five slices of pie for dessert.

Is there anyone who doesn't have a weakness for pie? Before the refrigerated crusts were available, a cook was often praised for their pie crusts. Pastry has lost out to convenience for most of us, but if you make your own crusts, here is a classic recipe from the Waldorf Astoria, circa 1917. This one uses 'vegetable shortening' which in the 30s in Greer County would likely be either lard or Crisco. Butter works well too.

Waldorf Astoria Pie Crust
Makes 2 9" crusts

¾ cup vegetable shortening

2 cups AP flour

Pinch salt

½ cup ice water

Cut shortening into the flour, using 2 forks, a pastry blender or a food processor. Keep working the dough until it looks like coarse meal. Stir the salt into the water and work into the flour shortening dough. Mix just until the dough forms a ball (you may not use all of the water, depending on humidity flour and temperature.) Divide in two parts and refrigerate one hour. Roll each out on a lightly floured board.

I have tremendous admiration for anyone who can bake well with a wood stove. I have cooked on one, and being able to move a pot around to different temperatures makes that pretty easy to learn. But I have helped people who could bake in a wood fired oven, and am still dazzled by the memory. A friend could put her open hand in an oven and guess the temperature within a few degrees, and had fine tuned keeping the fire even. I helped her with fruitcakes one year and they came out perfectly. Grandmother started with a wood stove in the kitchen when they bought the ranch in 1930, but propane soon followed. Not cutting wood to cook in July must have seemed like heaven.

Chess pie was always a favorite in our family. This recipe for lemon is especially good.

Lemon Chess Pie
1 pie

6 eggs

1 ¾ cups white sugar

3 Tablespoons melted butter

Pinch salt

½ teaspoon vanilla extract

½ cup lemon juice

Grated lemon zest for garnish

1 pie crust for 9" pan*

Preheat oven to 300 degrees. Place your crust in a pie pan and flute the edges. Set aside. In a bowl, beat eggs until their color lightens, about 5 minutes. Gradually beat in the remaining ingredients in order, up to the zest. Pour into the crust and bake for one hour, until well set and beginning to brown. Let cool then sprinkle lemon zest across the top.

*Try sprinkling a teaspoon of sugar on the pastry board when you roll out your dough. This helps it brown well.

You don't hear about vinegar pie often, but it was another one that could be constructed almost entirely out of a pantry. It starts with a blind baked crust, which is simply a crust that is baked empty. I have my granny's pie weights (other side of the family) and still use them. They are bean sized bits of porcelain that can tolerate high heat. Beans work as well, but just save the beans to use again, as once baked, they take forever to boil up. I know some bakers can just prick the crust well to keep it from bubbling up, but this has never worked for me. It still bubbles and there are holes for the filling to make the crust soggy. I have tried rice too, but ended up tearing the crust trying to make sure there were no grains left. Follow your heart. I usually blind bake at 350 degrees, and 10 minutes is usually right but keep an eye on it. You want the bottom brown, but if you go too long, the edges will burn when you bake it with the filling.

Vinegar Pie
Makes one pie

1 cup sugar

4 Tablespoons AP flour

1 cup cold water

3 egg yolks

1 whole egg

3 Tablespoons butter

½ cup cider vinegar

1 baked pie shell

3 egg whites

4 Tablespoons sugar

In a saucepan, whisk together the flour and sugar. Add cold water, continuing to whisk. Beat the egg and yolks in a separate bowl, adding the butter and vinegar. Stir into the sugar mixture, and cook over medium heat, stirring constantly, until it thickens, about 10 minutes. Pour into the pie shell and let cool. Preheat oven to 350 degrees. Move the oven rack to the middle of the oven. Beat the egg whites until stiff, then gradually add in the sugar to the meringue. Spread across the pie surface and bake until golden, 7-10 minutes.

Of course, there is pecan pie, pretty much everyone's favorite. While always traditional in the Southeast, I have eaten some fine examples of the delicacy in Oklahoma as well. This one is from a 1952 pamphlet from the home demonstration agency somewhere in Oklahoma. And it is 'pee-con' not 'pee-can,' at least in our family.

Pecan pie
Makes one pie

¼ cup butter, melted

1 cup sugar

¾ cup light corn syrup

3 eggs lightly beaten

1 teaspoon vanilla extract*

1 ¾ cups chopped pecans

1 unbaked pie crust, in a 9" pan

Preheat your oven to 350 degrees. Beat the butter, sugar and corn syrup together, then beat in the eggs and vanilla. Add the pecans, pour into the shell and bake 35 minutes or until well set.

- While Oklahoma entered the Union as a dry state, the occasional home distillery was not entirely unknown, especially once the oil boom started to bring in droves of thirsty young men. A creative baker might fine that a spoonful or two of some sort of booze (I like Bourbon in this) enhances the flavor mightily. Like the alcohol in the vanilla, it will evaporate before the pie is through baking, leaving just a hint of flavor.

One of my best memories of summertime in Oklahoma was picking strawberries. Being very young, and hence more flexible and closer to the ground, it was not the backbreaker for my sister and me that it was for the adults. We probably ate as many as we picked, but when we got home, we would have either strawberry shortcake or strawberry pie.

Strawberry Pie
Makes one pie

2 quarts fresh strawberries, washed and hulled

3 Tablespoons cornstarch

1 cup sugar

4 teaspoons lemon juice

1 9" baked pie crust

After washing, spread the berries out on towels to dry well. Divide in half, saving the prettiest ones. In a saucepan, crush the remaining berries to release the juice, adding the cornstarch and sugar and lemon juice. If you like, a few drops of red food coloring can go in now also. Cook, stirring over medium heat until it thickens, about 7 minutes. Arrange the reserved whole berries in the pie shell, heaping up in the center. Pour the cooked mixture over and refrigerate to set. Serve with whipped topping.

When I started talking about pulling this cookbook together, I asked my family what recipes they remember loving. My cousin David and Uncle Pete both thought immediately of an apple pie that baked in a brown bag. I finally found a recipe, which, I must say is pretty wonderful. Be certain that the brown paper bag you use is NOT recycled. Those seem to have a lower burning temperature, and yes, this is the voice of experience.

Apple Pie In A Bag
Makes one 9" pie

2 ½ pounds of apples, cored, peeled and quartered

1 cup sugar

2 Tablespoons plus ½ cup all purpose flour

¾ teaspoon ground cinnamon

¼ teaspoon ground nutmeg

¼ teaspoon ground ginger

1 9" unbaked pie shell laid in a pie pan

2 Tablespoons lemon juice

½ cup soft butter

Preheat oven to 375 degrees. Toss the apples with ½ of sugar, 2 Tablespoons flour, and the ground spices. Pour into the prepared pie crust, sprinkle with lemon juice and salt. Cream the remaining flour, sugar and salt with the softened butter. Spread over the apples. If you like a sprinkle of cinnamon and sugar can go on top. Place in a large, heavy brown bag and staple the open end closed. (Not recycled paper!) Bake for one hour. Let cool for at least fifteen minutes before you open the bag.

I mentioned fruitcake earlier. In the years before electricity came to the farm, any food that could be made and kept well was a treasure. My great grandmother Title, at the old house, had a spring under the granger, and could literally crawl under the building to put food to keep cool. (Just went and hugged my refrigerator, complete with ice maker and light. Imagining crawling into a dark hole in the ground as a necessity for feeding my family would mean a lot of grits.

So. Fruitcake. Even with all of the jokes, a lot of these get eaten around the holidays. This is a basic recipe, which can be varied infinitely. Certainly in the early days, more dried fruits were used, as in this recipe, but now the technicolor preserved fruits are more traditional. In this case, the high sugar content helps preserve the cakes. Fruitcakes were almost always made in bulk (this recipe yields 4 standard loaf pans) often around Thanksgiving, then wrapped in cheesecloth, and sprinkled with sherry or whiskey every couple of days, again to enhance preservation as well as keep the baker happy.

Thanksgiving Fruitcake
Makes four loaves

1 pound chopped pecans

3 ounces lemon extract (or whiskey)

2 pounds chopped dried fruit*

5 cups AP flour

1 pound butter

6 whole eggs

1 teaspoon baking powder

Soak the pecans in lemon extract or whiskey overnight in a glass container. Drain. Using ½ cup of the flour dust the chopped fruit and nuts. Preheat oven to 250 degrees. Heavily butter four loaf pans and dust with flour. Cream together the butter and sugar, then add the eggs one at a time, until completely blended. Sift together the remaining flour and baking powder, then add in the fruit and nuts, stirring to be sure they are evenly distributed. Bake for 2 1/3 to 3 hours, watching to make sure the edges don't burn. The cakes are done when a toothpick stuck in the middle comes out clean. Let cool for 30 minutes, then turn out on to a rack to finish cooling.

I have thought a lot about how hard my forbears worked just to survive. Everyone on the farm was focused on having enough food, father it was Papa Tittle working cattle or Mama Tittle canning. Something as simple as having coal available for heat to replace many hours of chopping wood must have felt like a miracle. But going back farther in Greer County history, I try to imagine hunting a buffalo while on foot, even in a group. Making a kill with a stone tipped spear or arrow must have meant being very close to the animal, and then butchering with napped flint knives. And I whine about cutting up a chicken.... The indigenous people contributed to foods in Oklahoma too. This is a recipe, handed down by a Cherokee grandmother.

Mixed Berry Crisp

½ cup rolled oats

½ cup AP flour

1 cup sugar more or less, depending on the sweetness of the berries

1/3 cup butter

½ teaspoon cinnamon

Mix ingredients well to a crumbly texture. Oil a cast iron skillet with more butter and add

4 cups of seasonal berries, washed and sliced as needed

Sprinkle the oat mixture over the berries and bake in a 350 ° oven for 20 minutes or until the top is golden brown.

Uncle Pete by the root cellar with admirers

I had never heard of oatmeal pie, but it is one of Uncle Pete's favorites.

Oatmeal Pie

1 pie crust store bought or homemade

4 eggs

Cup of sugar

3 Tablespoons flour

1 teaspoon ground cinnamon

Pinch salt

1 cup quick-cooking oats

1 cup corn syrup (or maple syrup)

½ stick melted butter

1 tablespoon vanilla extract

1 cup flaked coconut

Put the pastry in a 9"pie plate; crimp the edge. In a large bowl, combine eggs, sugar, flour, cinnamon and salt. Stir well, then add the salt, oats, corn syrup, butter and vanilla, stirring in well. Pour into pie crust, and top with shredded coconut. Bake at 350° for one hour, or until set. If the edge of the crust gets too dark, cover with foil for the last fifteen minutes of baking. Let cool and set, serve with vanilla ice cream if desired.

Chapter 4: Breakfast

'Oh what a beautiful morning, oh what a beautiful day,

I've got a beautiful feeling, everything's going my way.'

Mornings started before sunrise on the farm. Grandaddy's chair sat in the corner of the living room by the east window. When we heard him head to the chair from the kitchen, Yvonne and I could would groggily crawl out of bed so that we could race lacing and tying his boots. I don't remember who won, but I do remember that I usually had the right boot. Often we were also treated to a sunrise over the fields. We were usually there in the summer, so it was a cloudless dawn, but occasionally a stray cloud would gild itself. It was astounding how much we saw when there was no screen distraction.

Our room was just off the living room, where we shared a double bed next to the bathroom. I well remember the summer I was tall enough to reach the string to turn on the light in the bathroom. There was always a night light on, but full illumination is always the preference of a child in an unfamiliar house.

Grandmother would be up and dressed in the kitchen. There is some combination of bacon, sulfur matches, percolator coffee and a propane stove that I will catch a sniff of even now that puts me right back at the green formica table. Granddaddy was already out working by the time we kids ate. I remember bacon, eggs and toast and how wonderful white bought bread was, fried in the skillet the bacon had been cooked in and topped with a runny egg. Coyotes and the presence of a grocery store in town made keeping chickens a thing of the past, but I am sure it was the bacon fat flavor that made the eggs so delicious. The fat was scraped into a Folgers can that sat on the back of her stove, and I have often considered buying a can just to have the proper storage.

One element with farm breakfasts is speed. Granddaddy had milk cows in the late thirties and early forties, and a few cows bawling to be milked was a great motivator to eat and run. By the time we came along, cold cereal was the usual, but a sturdy meal was important for anyone with several hours of hard labor ahead before lunch. I remember a waffle iron, and pancakes occasionally. I think leftovers from dinner served often and my mother told me that Papa Tittle liked stale cornbread crumbled into buttermilk.

Perfect Cornbread
1 cup sifted AP flour

4 teaspoons baking powder

1 cup yellow corn meal

1 cup buttermilk

¼ cup sugar

¾ teaspoon salt

2 eggs

¼ cup soft shortening (or butter or bacon grease)

Sift the flour with the sugar, baking soda and salt. Stir in the cornmeal, and beat until just smooth. Don't over work it or your cornbread will be tough. Let the batter stand for a few minutes. Heat an iron skillet on the stove, and added a spoonful of oil to melt. Pour in the batter and bake in a 425° oven for 20-25 minutes or until golden on top.

Cornmeal was cheap, stored well and had lots of carbohydrates to fuel laborers. Cornbread came together much faster than yeasted doughs, but plenty of corn was eaten as grits. I would use a crockpot for this recipe, but a wood stove with a banked fire works just fine too.

Breakfast Grits

1 cup stone-ground grits or coarse cornmeal

Salt

¼ cup butter

Put the grits in a bowl, add water to cover by an inch and stir well. When it settles skim any floating chaff and debris and discard. Pour into a fine mesh strainer to drain. If you are using a crockpot, set it on high. Stir the drained grits, salt, butter and 5 cups of room temperature butter together. If you are using an oven start the grits in an oven proof pot with a lid, and set your oven at its lowest setting. Stir well, then either move into the oven or drop the crockpot to lowest setting and let cook for 8 hours, until creamy.

A hundred years ago, if you wanted sausage with your eggs for breakfast, you needed about a year's head start. In that time, a tiny piglet can transform to hams, bacon, sausage and chops enough to last a winter, the whole time consuming whatever leftovers didn't get eaten by the dogs. This highly efficient system has worked for humans for 13,000 years. I have helped with a feral hog butchering twenty years ago, and can attest that it is a staggering amount of work, even with readily available refrigeration and electricity. Imaging what it was like when the tools were a sharp knife, a rifle, a wood fire and a wash tub is daunting. Being involved from the beginning with raising and harvesting food gives a unique connection that I miss. But a long November day in the cold taking a 400 pound hog down to wrapped chops I don't miss!

Sausage is universal, a way to use every morsel of the beast, 'from tail to grunt'. Bulk breakfast sausage is the easiest, and can be replicated in modern kitchens. I like this recipe, a little spicy, and an easy recipe to multiply and freeze. Ask your butcher to grind together pork shoulder and enough fat to bring it to 70% lean. This recipe works fine with other meats, like turkey or venison. Just make sure the butcher adds enough pork fat to the grind to make it 30% fat, or it will be tough and dry and not cook properly.

Breakfast Sausage
12 patties

2 bay leaves

1-3 teaspoons red chili flakes

¼ cup finely chopped fresh sage

2 teaspoons freshly ground nutmeg*

1 ½ Tablespoons salt

1-3 teaspoons ground black pepper

2 pounds ground pork

Combine the spices in a grinder or mortar and pestle and grind to a powder. Add to the pork and mix with your hands until the spice mix is evenly distributed. Cook a teaspoonful in a hot skillet and taste to check seasonings, adjust as needed. Refrigerate for at least an hour overnight is better.

I use an ice cream scoop and a muffin tin to form the patties. Put a small square of plastic wrap into the muffin tin, add a level scoop of sausage, pack down and twist the plastic tightly to seal.. Then another piece of plastic wrap and so on. Freeze in the tin, then take them out and move them to a zip lock bag and return to the freezer. You can also partially fry them before freezing and just quickly microwave to serve.

*Fresh nutmeg may seem frivolous, but the whole nutmegs are very available over the Internet, and last forever. Once it is ground the flavor disappears so quickly that you might as well use floor sweep.

I can eat a lot of sausage, but it helps to think of it as a condiment. Sausage gravy then, is the natural progression. Traditionally, this goes over biscuits, but is equally good over grits or even chicken fried steak.

Sausage Gravy

½ pound pork sausage

3 Tablespoons flour

1 can evaporated milk*

Black pepper

In a hot cast iron skillet, cook the sausage, breaking it into small pieces, until it is well browned. Sprinkle the flour over the meat, a bit at a time, stirring to let it cook out the 'raw' flavor. When it is browned, start to add the milk slowly over medium heat, letting it thicken. You may need less than the can of milk; get it to a texture you like, and if you need more liquid, water or regular milk works.

Add black pepper to taste and serve.

Another fine contribution from Mexico is chorizo. Fine tune the seasonings to suit yourself, and if you are a chilihead, consider grinding fresh jalapenos in with the meat.

Mexican Chorizo Sausage
Yields a scant two pounds

½ cup dried powdered chilies*

1/2 cup finely chopped fresh cilantro

2 Tablespoons apple cider vinegar

1 Tablespoon paprika

1 Tablespoon salt

2 teaspoons oregano

2 teaspoons ground black pepper

1 ½ teaspoons ground cumin

½ teaspoon granulated garlic powder

1 ½ pounds 70% lean ground pork

Place everything but the pork in a blender or grind by hand. Add to the meat and hand mix until the spices are evenly distributed.

I pack this in ½ pound portions and freeze. It is great for breakfast tacos. Cook the meat in a skillet over medium heat, breaking it up and browning it well. Add 4-6 eggs, drop the heat to low and cook until set. Serve on tortillas, topping with cheese if you like.

*I use guajillo chilies and canned chipotles. The smokiness is very nice.

Another nice way to use the sausage, which would certainly do well in tacos is chorizo con papas. Have ½ pound chorizo cooked and crumbled, set aside. Without washing the pan, cook ½ cup of chopped onion and ½ pound cooked potatoes, cut in slices. Add a bit of oil or fat if needed, and let the potatoes brown well. Add the cooked chorizo and serve.

Biscuits were a real test of a cook's skills, especially over an open fire. The advent of Bisquick and 'whomp' biscuits (the ones in the tube) leveled that field. There is a somewhat apocalyptic story told in my family about Papa Tittle. He was a foreman for the JayBuckle Ranch in the 1880s and drove herds to Kansas and Fort Worth for sale. No one liked having to cook for a hungry crew of complaining cowhands after a very long days work, so the tradition became that, in the absence of a hired cook, whoever complained last became the new 'Cookie.' Apparently one fellow had gotten very tired of the job and added about a cup of salt to the biscuits one morning. Papa Tittle took a bite and said: 'Lordie these biscuits are salty!!' and realizing the consequences, finished with: 'Just the way I like them!'

Traditionally the fat is cut into the flour and baking powder with a couple of forks or a pastry blender. I find the easiest way is to freeze the butter or shortening   (or lard for the sake of authenticity and flavor) and then grating it by hand or with a food processor and quickly stirring it in to the flour mixture.

Biscuits
2 cups AP flour

4 teaspoons baking powder

½ teaspoon salt

4 ounces fat frozen and grated*

1cup buttermilk

Preheat your oven at 450°. In a bowl, sift together the flour, baking soda and salt, then add the frozen fat and stir quickly. (Don't use your hands, as you want the fat to distribute evenly while still frozen, not melted.) Stir as little as possible then quickly stir in the buttermilk, again working the dough as little as possible, and let rest for ten minutes.

Turn the dough out on a floured surface, and roll out to 1" thick. Using a 2" cutter, or juice glass, push down through the dough and place the biscuits on a baking sheet or in a cast iron skillet so the sides just touch. Form leftover dough into a twist and bake alongside. The second working of the dough toughens it, and a different shape helps identify. Brush with melted butter if you like and bake for 17 minutes or so, checking at fifteen. They are done when they are golden brown.

If you add 1/2cup of sugar and increase the buttermilk as necessary, these make dandy shortcakes for strawberries. Add some grated cheese if you like.

Chapter Five: We've got game

"Many a new day will dawn,

Many a red sun will set,

Many a blue moon will shine.'

Gathering as much information as I can for this has me on the phone to Uncle Pete often. I was trying to get a clear image of life in Greer County early in the twentieth century, gathering mundanities, and asked: 'What kind of wood did you all cut for heat?' His reply: 'Whatever burned.' Food seemed to be much the same after the Great Depression. You ate whatever was slow enough to catch. Hunting was a part of life there and then, as much as a commute to work is now. Deer and quail were around, an occasional hog perhaps, but a great deal of the stew pot was filled with squirrel and possum and rabbit. Eventually there was a meat locker in Granite where a larger animal could be stored, but as I mentioned in the last chapter, there is a tremendous amount of work between a deer on the hoof and venison on a plate. I have butchered chickens from squawk to table, and five pounds of meat took me the best part of a day. And not nearly as much fun as you might think.

One Christmas time when all the cousins were at the house in Granite, Pete decided to take us 'wolf hunting.' We piled in the back of Granddaddy's red pickup truck and drove out to the South pasture. There was some starlight, perhaps, but no moon, and Pete knew the dirt road well enough to drive without lights the last bit. He cautioned us to be quiet, and I am pretty sure had a shotgun in the rack, and reassured us that he wouldn't let the wolves take us. All five of us were terrified and bluffing, and in ten minutes, we began to see green eyes glowing. First one pair, but we were soon surrounded by six wolves. Pete was shaking, and we were too. Then one of the wolves mooed. And we realized that Pete was shaking with laughter.

Back at the house we were telling Mother and Aunt Frances about seeing wolves, and although Grandmother knew better, they both lit into Pete. Pretty sure that was the best part for him.

Rabbit was more common around Greer County, and a welcome source of protein. They were plentiful, easy to clean, and tasty. The meat is very lean, and dries out easily, so braising or pan frying with gravy work well. This also lets you stretch the meat out with some vegetables, and serve with potatoes. Most of us buy our bunnies now, and a butcher can cut it up for you. If you are a hunter, you already know how. This recipe starts the day before you want to serve it.

Braised Rabbit
Serves 3-4

1 rabbit cut into 8 pieces

½ cup mustard

Salt and pepper

Fat for frying*

1 ½ cups broth*

1 large onion, chopped

1 cup sliced mushrooms

3 cloves garlic, chopped

4 Tablespoons butter

4 Tablespoons flour

2 teaspoons chopped fresh sage or ½ teaspoon dried

1 teaspoon fresh thyme, chopped

2 ½ cups liquid**

1/2cup mustard

The evening before you plan to serve the rabbit, rinse the pieces well, pat dry, then rub with the mustard to cover thickly. Salt and pepper liberally, more than you think you will need. This is a moist brine and the salt is there to tenderize, but won't make it overly salty. Store the rabbit in the refrigerator in a plastic bag for 8 hours and up to twelve.

Heat your oven to 350°. Rinse the rabbit again and pat dry. Heat ½" oil in a skillet and brown the rabbit on both sides in batches, careful not to crowd the pan. Move the pieces to an ovenproof, lidded casserole and pour the broth in, cover and put in the oven for fifteen minutes. In the unrinsed skillet, cook the onion and mushrooms until brown, scraping the pan and adding more fat as needed. When they begin to brown, turn the heat to low and add the garlic and butter. Cook just until you can smell the garlic, then toss in the flour, still stirring to brown the flour. As it thickens, gradually add the liquid and mustard. Cook over low heat until reduce by one third, then pour over the rabbit, replace the cover and return to the oven for 45 minutes or until the rabbit is tender.

This is best when it has been cooled and allowed to rest for a few hours to let the flavors meld. Reheat in the oven then put the rabbit pieces on a deep serving platter. Taste the gravy, season as needed and if the gravy seems then, cook it to reduce and pour over the meat.

*The type of oil you use will flavor the meat, and it is best if it pairs with the broth. For example, for a mild dish, where the herb flavors dominate, use a neutral oil and chicken broth. For more richness, lard and a ham broth is delicious. Even olive oil with tomato juice is an option, and white wine is always good. Use your imagination and your nose.

**You can use milk, wine, water, broth or a mixture. Our ancestors used what they had, and came up with some amazing dishes- look through your cabinets for inspiration.

My dad hunted jackrabbits and I remember them fondly. We also had dove, which can be cooked the same way you did the rabbit. But the best recipe for dove I earned from an old cowboy, although he was a Texan. But Greer County was in Texas almost as long as it was in Oklahoma, so we'll let this one slide. These were done over a campfire, but a grill or 350° oven work too. And you can't get much easier than this.

Butch's Dove Poppers

Serves four

16 dove breast halves

8 strips bacon, halved

jalapenos cut in strips

1 cup peach jam

3 Tablespoons horseradish or to taste

Toothpicks

Rinse and dry the dove breasts and place on a platter. Take each breast half, and add jalapeno strips to taste, wrap in bacon and pin with the toothpick. Grill or bake until the bacon is crisp. Mix the jam and horseradish and serve on the side for dipping.

Possum meat is a different story. I know people who have eaten it, and it supposedly tastes like chicken, but what doesn't? In Texas we refer to armadillo as 'possum on the half shell,' but I have yet to meet anyone who has sampled armadillo. This is a Cherokee recipe for possum, which I am told is traditional.

The trick is to catch a live possum. Then you feed him for two weeks, good clean food like table scraps and bread to fatten him. Make sure he has plenty of fresh water. Butcher, skin and clean him, then soak in a salt brine (1/2 cup salt to 2 quarts water) for twenty four hours in the refrigerator.

Cherokee Possum

1 possum, cleaned and brined

3 pounds sweet potatoes cut into 2" chunks

1 teaspoon chopped fresh sage

1 Tablespoon butter

Salt and pepper

1 cup cider

Place the possum on an oiled cookie sheet, season with salt and pepper inside and out. Rub the interior cavity with butter, then sage. Fill with sweet potato chunks, heaping any extras around. Pour cider over all and bake in a slow, 275° oven for 3-4hours or until the potatoes and possum are tender.

My friend then commented: 'You can throw out the Possum, but the sweet potatoes are good.'

Somewhere in the closet in the dining room at the farm there are two cigar boxes full of rattlesnake rattles. That is one animal that has always been quite abundant there. Granddaddy saved the rattles, and every time I think of it, I want to beg Pete for them and string them like popcorn for a Christmas tree. The story goes that some Church Ladies were visiting once and asked about them; "Did you really kill all those snakes, Mr. Stimson?" He replied that no, he didn't, he just caught them and relieved them of their rattles, because they are very polite animals and won't strike if they can't rattle first. The response is lost to history.

In the seventies I spent a couple of summers cooking for an archaeology camp in northern Arizona. In the ten weeks of the dig, we killed seventeen snakes, all identical. It was sponsored by Arizona State University, so the baby archeologists were students, most from the northeast, so every time we caught one (and they were good sized, between 38 and 42 inches) darn if I didn't get requests to cook them. After the first one, I had learned to agree if the captor would dress and skin them. We gad fried rattlesnake appetizers, and then the vertebrae were boiled clean for necklaces. The plate always came back clean, I believe a function of Yankees wanting to truthfully say they ate rattlesnake over the summer and starving grad students who would happily eat anything.

Of course, rattlesnake is reputed to taste like chicken, but to me, it was quite gamey, and much more like frog legs. I worked for several years at a high end grocery that served frozen rattlesnake meat, and learned that to legally sell it, it had to be 'farmed.' I have to wonder what that looked like? Several people shared recipes. Many were just snake, simmered to make deboning easier, then substituted for a less exotic meat in something like chili or pasta sauce. I suspect that the main ingredient was not revealed until all of the guests had at least sampled the dish. I do remember one older gentleman who laughed about the 'farmed' snake and said that it didn't have any flavor. He recommended getting your own, fresh, but to make sure you cut the head off before getting it near the kitchen. He didn't debone, just let everyone deal with it as they ate. This is his recipe, and I wish I could remember his name.

Rattlesnake Ragout

1 ½ pounds cleaned, skinned snake cut in 3" sections

2 Tablespoons butter

2 chopped jalapenos

1 chopped red onion

2 cloves garlic

2 cups whole milk

2 Tablespoons Madeira (optional)

Salt and pepper

Chopped scallions and lime wedges for garnish

Place the snake pieces in a baking dish and dot with the butter. Sprinkle the peppers, garlic and onions evenly, and add the milk and Madeira. Salt and pepper and bake at 325° until tender, about 50 minutes to an hour. Serve with rice.

Venison is one of the game dishes that we see as exotic but delicious. I remember seeing white tail deer around Granite but not for a long time. The earlier sausage recipes work beautifully with deer meat, but I suspect that most deer got cooked into a stew by the indigenous people and later by my ancestors. Lots of mouths to feed can sure make you creative. I like this recipe because it makes use of the lesser parts, the neck and cheeks. Nothing beats a grilled venison back strap, but this is sustenance cooking at its best.

Venison Pie

3 pounds venison bones, meat attached (neck, cheeks, trimmings)

1 quart water

2 Tablespoons cider vinegar

½ cup chopped celery (lots of leaves)

1 cup chopped carrot

1 cup chopped onion

Salt and pepper

½ cup flour

3 Tablespoons butter

1 teaspoon fresh thyme or two good pinches dried

Uncooked pie crust or biscuits

¼ cup milk

Place the venison, carrots, celery and onions in a crockpot with the water and vinegar. Cover and cook for two hours or until the meat is falling of the bone. Remove from the broth, cool, and separate the meat from the bones, reserving the broth. Put the meat into an oiled baking dish. Preheat your oven to 425°. In a skillet melt the butter and stir in the flour, cooking over low heat until it begins to brown. Add the broth with vegetables a ladleful at a time, stirring as it thickens. When thick, add the thyme, pour over the meat, cover with the crust, brush with the milk and bake for ten minutes or until the crust is golden.

Most of us have had jerky, usually from a convenience store, saturated with lord knows what and encased in plastic, but the origins of this noble recipe goes back at least 12,000 years. Mammoth in Europe were preserved by salting, smoking and brining strips for later use, and without jerky, surviving the last ice age would certainly have been tougher. In Alaska, I have seen salmon jerky made, but for our plains Indians in Oklahoma, the animal of choice would be buffalo.

This is an easy recipe, and beef brisket substitutes just fine for buffalo meat. I usually prefer fewer seasonings, but this recipe is a blank palate. Tweak it to your heart's delight. Soy sauce, BBQ sauce, Worcestershire sauce, liquid smoke can all settle nicely into the marinade. My friend Ben over in Alabama even puts a splash of bourbon in his, but that's Alabama. This is an easy recipe, but does take time, and as we know this keeps just fine, so make quite a bit at once. A cheap, lean boneless cut works best; I prefer brisket. When you get it home, and unwrap it, you will usually find a good fat cap covering one side. This bastes the meat when you roast it, but for jerky, you need to remove as much fat as possible. Don't throw it out, though. Your Grandmother would have rendered it for tallow to cook with, highly recommended, and at the very least, your dogs will thank you. I have yet to see a cholesterol phobic dog.

Oven Beef Jerky
Beef brisket, trimmed of fat

Salt and pepper

Apple cider vinegar

Honey

Hot sauce (optional)

I do this the easy way, and slice the meat into manageable chunks, then freeze for an hour or so. Take one piece out at a time and slice between 1/4" and ½" thick in strips. Cut <u>across</u> the grain. Pack the strips in a plastic zip lock bag or other sealable container. Make your marinade. I use ¼ cup each of salt, pepper and honey, ½ cup vinegar and as much hot sauce as you like. Pour over the brisket and add water to cover. Refrigerate. Every hour take it out and shake it and give it a little massage. Four hours is about right, but not more than ten.

This can get messy, so line the bottom of your oven with foil. My convection oven can go as low as 170°, which works fine. I use a rimmed baking pan and a cooling rack and line the pan with foil as well. Pull out enough strips to cover the rack, drain them and pat them dry. Put the cooling rack over the baking sheet and load it up, leaving ½" between the strips for air to circulate. If you end up liking this project, investing in some extra racks speeds things up, or you can use your oven racks: spray them with a cooking spray and hang the strips on like you are drying socks.

Set your oven as low as it can go and slide the jerky in. I block the door open with a dish towel, which improves circulation but if you use a convection oven this isn't necessary. Three full racks take about 4-5 hours. When you think it is done, take a piece out and let it cool completely. It should be stiff, and when held by one end, not flop over. It is difficult to overcook jerky (although I have...) but easy to undercook it and even with the salt, any moisture can quickly lead to mold.

You can eat this right away, but leave it out overnight, or better, a full 24 hours so that it is completely dry. Seal or wrap in foil, and store in the freezer indefinitely.

Given the work involved to get food on the table, a day spent by a lake, under a shade tree with a fishing pole must have been bliss. There were catfish of course, in most of the lakes and rivers, and 'pan fish' like crappie, bluegill and sunfish in the farm ponds and lakes. These are small, often boney fish, and it took quite a few to make a meal. Cleaning, deboning or fileting and skinning or scaling took time, but was doubtless a welcome break in routine. Catfish, being larger, were often the centerpiece at church dinners, usually fried with hush puppies. This is how I remember the bluegill and crappie being cooked.

Pan Fish Fry
Feeds 4

8-12 small fish, gutted, scaled and heads removed

Large bowl of ice water with ¼ cup salt added

1 egg, beaten

1 can evaporated milk

Cornmeal or commercial fry mix

Salt and pepper

'Cajun Seasoning' (optional)

½ stick butter melted

As you clean the fish, drop them into the iced salt water to chill. Set your oven for 375°. Cover one or two baking sheets with foil for easy clean up. Combine the milk and egg, beating well. Drain the ice water from the fish then toss with the egg/milk wash. Pour 2 cups of cornmeal or mix into a zip lock gallon size bag or paper bag. Drain the milk from the fish, then toss with the cornmeal to cover well.

Brush the foil covered baking sheet with melted butter. Take each fish from the meal, shaking well to remove excess, and lay out on the pan. Brush well with butter and bake for 3-4 minutes, then turn them over, baste again with the butter, and return to the oven for another 3-4 minutes. The baking time will depend on the size of the fish. It is done when it breaks up easily with a fork.

Serve with lemon and hot sauce. The skin and tail will be crunchy, and the bones are removed easily by breaking the fish open and pulling out the spine.

Vegetables like corn on the cob or par boiled potatoes can go in the oven at the same time.

The same recipe works well for catfish, just increase the cooking time as needed.

Chapter six: Putting food by

"Chicks and ducks and geese better scurry"

As I gathered memories and recipes from my family, the one thing everyone mentioned was Grandmother's pickled peaches. These were treasures, and hoarded all year until the next summer when the next crop came in. I have no idea how many quarts she put up every year to keep all the kids and grandkids supplied, but I could have eaten a cellar full all by myself. I probably still could. I haven't found her recipe, but this one comes very close, and when the Fredricksberg peaches come in next year I will be using it. She always pickled them peeled but whole, seed in, which I believe enhances the flavor. You'll need wide mouthed quart canning jars. You will also need a canner- a pot large enough to hold the quarts submerged in boiling water to seal them. If you don't have one, make a smaller batch and refrigerate. You can freeze them, but the texture will change a lot.

Jennie's Pickled Peaches
Makes four-five quarts

4 pounds fresh ripe peaches

4 cups sugar

1 ½ cup cider vinegar

1 cup water

½ teaspoon salt

1 teaspoon vanilla extract

Whole cloves

5 cinnamon sticks

To peel the peaches, start a large pan of water boiling, and cut an X on the bottom of each peach, just through the skin. Submerge the peaches, for about a minute, cool and the peel should slip off. The X you cut will give you a place to start.

In a large pot, combine the sugar, vinegar, water, salt and vanilla and bring to a boil for five minutes. Lower the heat to medium low, just below a simmer. Put several whole cloves in each peach and add to the syrup. Cook until tender, about 25 minutes.

While the peaches cook, sterilize your jars. Dishwashers do a good job now, or just get the water boiling in the canner and boil the jars, lids and tops for five minutes. When the peaches are done, spoon them into the jars, add a cinnamon stick and top with the syrup to ½" from the rim. Wipe the rims well, add the lids and rings. Process for 10 minutes in boiling water to seal. When you take them out, place them lid side down on a clean towel to form the vacuum seal.

I have tweaked her recipe little. Here in Texas, we end up with a lot of less than perfect peaches- under ripe, sometimes in a rainy year, kind of spongy and sometimes perfectly fine, just a little on the homely side. I like to mix sweet and savory, and this cooks up a lot like a non-tomato barbecue sauce, which is what I use it for.

Elaine's Spicy Peach Ketchup

1 pound of peaches, peeled, seeds removed and chopped coarsely

1 cup sugar

1 cup white wine, 1 cup water or

2 cups water

1 Tablespoon homemade pickling mix*

2 Tablespoons chopped red onion

2 Tablespoons oil

Salt and pepper to taste

Mix the sugar and water (and wine if you like) in a saucepan and bring to a simmer, stirring to dissolve the sugar. Add the pickling spice and let steep for an hour, until cool. Strain out the spice, and move back to the saucepan. Add the peaches, bring to a boil and drop to a simmer for 5 minutes, until just soft. Drain off the liquid. In a small pan, saute the onions in the oil over low heat just until soft. Add to the peach mixture and stir well. Serve cold as a relish with meats, or puree as a sauce.

*Pickling spice: heat a heavy skillet over medium heat. Pull off the stove and add ½ teaspoon each: Allspice berries, cumin seeds, peppercorns, dried red chilies, coriander seeds, mustard seeds and 2 bay leaves. Stir and let them toast, off the heat. By the time the skillet has cooled they are done, and this is the only way I have found I can do them and manage not to burn them.

Another fond food memory was Grandmother's candied orange and grapefruit peels at Christmas time. I have a very early memory from around five years old, of the exact scent when Mother opened the cookie tin Grandmother had sent home with us from Thanksgiving. It smells more like Christmas to me than anything. I was delighted to find, a few years later, that this was the easiest recipe I would ever see. If you can, get organic fruit, or scrub the rinds very well to get rid of insecticide residue.

Candied Citrus Peel

4 large pink grapefruit

2 ½ cups granulated sugar

With a vegetable peeler, remove the colored peel from the grapefruits in strips, getting as little of the white pith as possible. Put the peels in a saucepan and cover with cold water, bring to a boil and drain. Cover with cold water again and repeat twice more- a total of three times. In the same pan, mix two cups of sugar with one cup of water, bring to a simmer, add the peels and simmer over low heat for 20 minutes or until translucent. Let them cool for ten minutes, then remove them to a rack to dry, using tongs or a slotted spoon. Dry for 3-4 hours, roll in the rest of the sugar, and package in cookie tins lined with Christmas paper, or just plastic bags. Dip ½ of each strip in melted chocolate if you like, let harden and package.

I don't remember a lot of jams and jellies on the farm, but I remember helping put some up. This recipe is from a friend, who was raised near there. Like me, she associates grapefruit season with the holidays. The salt seems odd in here, but it is used more like cranberry sauce to accompany meats, which makes more sense.

Grapefruit Cranberry Marmalade

1 pound raw fresh cranberries

2 large ruby grapefruit, scrubbed

2 cups water

2 teaspoons sea salt

3 cups sugar

Chop the grapefruit very coarsely. I like to slice it into quarters and then thinly slice to make it pretty, but chunks are fine. About the size of the last joint on your pinkie figure is ideal. In a heavy pot like a dutch oven, put all of the ingredients but the sugar, bring to a boil over medium high heat reduce the heat to low, cover and simmer for fifteen minutes. Let cool, then refrigerate overnight.

Sterilize your jars, rings and lids and get your canner ready. (again, if you don't have a caner, this can keep well in the refrigerator for a couple of weeks.) Put the pot with the cranberry and grapefruit mixture back on the stove, over medium high heat, add the sugar and stir to dissolve. Bring to a boil, uncovered, stirring occasionally so it doesn't have a chance to burn. Boil for 10-12 minutes, letting it thicken. Remove from the heat and let cool. Taste and adjust salt and sugar if needed. Ladle into jars, wipe the rims well and seal with lids and rings. Process submerged in boiling water for 10 minutes. Remove from the water and invert on a clean towel to seal.

I have often seen pepper jelly poured over a slab of cream cheese and served with crackers as an appetizer. Usually served in the living room, keeping kids out of the kitchen and dining room. I am thinking the marmalade recipe above would be good served that way, and it reminded me of Jezebel sauce which I remember being served with ham. I am making myself hungry...

Jezebel Sauce

1 pint jar apple jelly

1 pint jar pineapple preserves

½ cup prepared horseradish

¼ cup dry mustard

1 Tablespoon coarsely ground black pepper

Mix all of the ingredients together until well blended. Cover and refrigerate for 24 hours before serving. Keeps for two weeks, refrigerated.

Most people have little use for okra, but it grows beautifully in the hot dry Oklahoma summers. We would occasionally eat it fried in bacon fat with a cornmeal crust, but what isn't delicious cooked that way? Pickled, though, is when okra can really shine.

Pickled Okra
Makes four pints

2 pounds smallest okra pods

1 teaspoon dried red pepper flakes

2 teaspoons mustard seed

1 teaspoon dried dill

4 whole, peeled cloves of garlic

4 dried red chili pods

1 teaspoon whole black pepper corns

3 Tablespoons sea salt

2 cups cider vinegar

2 cups water

Wash and trim the okra, leaving ¼" stems. Sterilize 4 wide mouth pint jars, rings and lids. Divide the spices evenly amongst the jars, then pack with the okra. Alternating stems and tails makes them fit best. Bring the vinegar, water and salt to a boil, and pour over the okra, to within ¼" of the rim. Top the jars with lids and rings and invert to seal. Store for 2 days before eating.

Not one of Grandmother's recipes, but I remember buying a pint jar of it somewhere in Altus, and the taste always reminds me of July on Oklahoma. When I was young, watermelons still had seeds and all the kids could spit them, but nowhere near as far as Granddaddy. He always called the striped variety 'rattlesnake melons' and was very suspicious of the new yellow meat ones. He called them mealy. There used to be a huge elm in the front yard, and fireflies and chiggers. I imagined that after a mid-summer visit from all of the grandkids, after the next rain, most of that lawn sprouted with baby watermelon plants. Granddaddy also put salt and pepper on his melon, which I find as an adult, is my preference too. Maybe even a little hot sauce.

I made watermelon pickles once, and they disappeared very quickly. An excellent accompaniment to fried chicken. Many kitchen chores at the farm were done in the shade of a sycamore beside the kitchen porch. I would highly suggest that as a spot for cleaning the watermelon rind, and have a hose handy. By the time I had six pints canned, it looked like I had butchered a pig in the kitchen.

Homesteaders, 1940

Watermelon Pickles
Makes 4 quarts

Rind from a small watermelon

1 ½ cup cider vinegar

3 cups water

1/3 cup pickling spice

2 cups sugar

1 teaspoon salt

Red Hot Candies (optional)

Remove all of the meat from the watermelon and cut in strips. Using a vegetable peeler, remove the skin, leaving only the white rind, and cut into bite sized pieces. In a large saucepan or dutch oven, bring the vinegar, water, salt, spice and sugar to a boil. Lower the heat and simmer for ten minutes. Take off of the stove Add the prepared rind, cover and let sit for 4-6 hours, stirring occasionally to make sure all the pieces soak evenly.

Sterilize wide mouth half pint jars, rings and lids in boiling water. Ladle the pickles into the jars, then bring the syrup back to a boil and pour over the pickles, filling to ¼" from the rim. Add a few of the candies for color and a little bite. Wipe the rims and seal. Refrigerate.

Mother's favorite fruit was I think plums, although she and Frances and Grandmother could probably have been quite content as fruitarians. I suspect growing up when fruit was unavailable so much of the year made it very special for them. Mother loved the blue Italian plums and made jam every year. It went to Granite with us at Christmas to barter for our supply of pickled peaches. Nothing is better on hot corn bread. I found this recipe slipped into an old cookbook, and recognized her handwriting.

Bobbie's Plum Jam
Makes 8 half-pint jars

4 pounds plums

3 cups water

6 cups sugar

1 teaspoon ground cinnamon

1 teaspoon ground ginger

2 ounces fruit pectin (Certo liquid)

Boil a large pot of water and blanch the plums for one minute. Drain and let cool, then remove the peels and seeds and any stems. Chop the fruit into large dice. Return the diced plums to the pot, add the water and cook over medium, at a simmer until they are tender, 7-10 minutes. Stir to break up fhte flesh, and simmer another few minutes, then drain. Return to the pot, add the plums, sugar, cinnamon and ginger and cook just at a simmer for 20 minutes or so, until it thickens. Slowly add the pectin and stir in well to evenly distribute. Boil for 1 minute, stirring constantly. Let cool and pour into sterilized jars. (This doesn't have enough acid to keep well, so refrigerate)

While not a pickle, this salad was always one of my favorites. I have tweaked it over the years, but remember having it or something like it often in the early summer at Grandmother's. I seem to remember that Granddaddy added a good splash of Trappey's pepper vinegar to his.

Cucumber Salad

2 cucumbers

1 large sweet onion

! teaspoon salt

2 cups cherry tomatoes

Chopped fresh parsley, basil or a combination

½ cup white vinegar

1 teaspoon ground pepper

1 teaspoon honey

Peel the cucumbers if you like. If they are bought cucumbers, either scrub very well or peel, because there is often a wax used to preserve them that isn't good for us. Grandmother often 'peeled' hers using a fork to cut stripes lengthwise, so when the cucumber was sliced, it had a frilled edge. Slice the cucumber evenly in ¼" slices. Peel the onion, cut in quarters from stem to root, then slice in ¼" pieces.

Put the onions and cucumbers in a bowl and toss well with the salt. Top with ice and cover. Refrigerate overnight.

Drain the salad, and rinse well, then return to the bowl. Half the tomatoes and add along with the remaining ingredients, toss well and return to the refrigerator for at least an hour before serving.

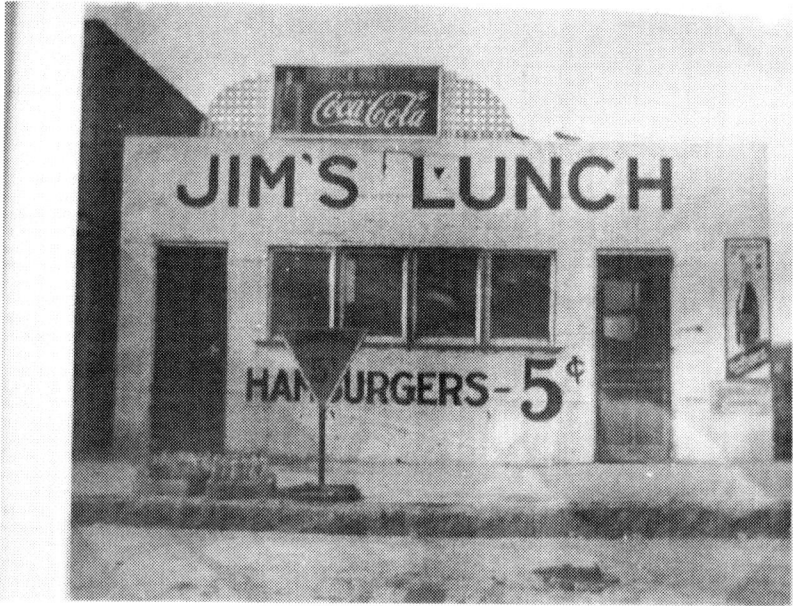

Chapter Seven: Stewin'

'Oh the farmer and the cowman should be friends.

One man likes to push a plow, one man likes to chase a cow,

But there's no reason they cain't be friends.'

Braising and stewing are ideal for days when you can't stand at a stove the whole time, which is pretty much always for farmers and ranchers. It brings out the best in cheap and tough cuts, like the brisket left over when the steaks are sold and the chicken who isn't hitting quota with her egg production. A little protein and a lot of starch and vegetables go much farther than a fried chicken or steak dinner. It is a testament to Oklahoma hospitality that frying a chicken for Sunday dinner was traditional if the preacher was coming to eat. Only young and tender chickens can be fried which meant sacrificing a potential layer's production years or supporting a worthless rooster, who was probably keeping a ruckus going in the henhouse, until he was either big enough or obnoxious enough to butcher. Is it politically incorrect to think there might be a lesson there?

Sam Houston Tittle was Sheriff in Greer County. My mother told this story many times. Papa Tittle was having dinner with one of the chiefs in his territory and his family. He commented on how delicious the stew was, while helping himself to another serving. Mrs. Chief replied: 'Dig deep, puppy in bottom.' Not our taste now, but I suspect that was a very gracious invitation then. The story stuck with us as these things often do, and whenever someone served themselves seconds at Mother's table, they were told: 'Dig deep, puppy in bottom.' Now I suspect that served her well as a savings on groceries, and always got a quizzical look, at best.

I am sure there is a recipe out there for puppy stew, so check the Internet, you won't find it here. While roasting was likely an accident, the discovery of the improved flavor and digestibility of cooked foods, braising had to be a deliberate act. As a card-carrying womanist, it doesn't surprise me in the least that men seem to have a chromosomal attachment to roasting and the grill and open flames, but it was us ladies who put together the essentials of a good braise. It allowed us to wean babies younger, and to keep the sick and elderly nourished. It also kept women close to a hearth, and safety, as well as convenience and warmth. Let the boys stand around outside in the weather, shooing saber toothed tigers, I'll take my kitchen any day.

Short of tossing a slab of meat on a grill, braising is about as simple as it gets. There are three or four steps, but from them whole cuisines have grown. Here is a basic recipe, another blank canvas for improvisation.

Pot Roast

6-10 servings, freezes well

1 -4 to 5 pound chuck roast or brisket

Salt and pepper

Oil

1 cup each chopped carrot and chopped celery

2 cups chopped onion

1-2 cups red wine or water

1-2 cups beef stock

Salt and pepper the roast, using at least twice as much seasoning as you think you need. This is a big piece of meat. If you have time, wrap it in plastic wrap and let it sit in the refrigerator for an hour or more, up to a day.[1] Unwrap it, pat it dry with paper towels. In a heavy skillet, heat the oil over medium heat and brown every side of the meat. Move to a crockpot, or an ovenproof pot with a lid. Turn the heat to medium low. Slow cook the carrots, onions and celery just until they are softened, but not browned. Add to the meat in the crockpot. Turn off the heat, and pour the wine or water into the hot skillet, stirring to loosen any tasty bits from the bottom. Pour over the meat and vegetables, then repeat with the beef stock. Turn the crockpot on low, cover and walk away. Alternatively, set your oven at 170°, and put the covered pot in the oven.

Come back in 8-10 hours, to a well perfumed house and dinner. You will also have plenty of leftovers.

There is no limit to how you can tweak this to your taste. You are in charge, remember, not that fancy schmancy guy on the Food Channel.

Sometimes you will want to add some flavors that can't stand up to such a long cook, or even some that you simply want to keep intact. Carrots cooked into the original pot roast are complimented by a couple of handfuls of baby carrots added a half hour before you serve. Potatoes, cut in bite sized pieces can be added, or mushrooms, pearl onions, tomatoes, turnips, really anything else that you have on hand the genius of home cooking is improvisation. Do gauge the cooking time from the density and size of whatever you add. Frozen peas, corn or well rinsed canned beans can be stirred in at the very last minute. So can spinach, chard, kale, or that bag of coleslaw mix you were wondering what to do with. Ask the farmer at the farmer's market or the produce expert at the grocery what would fit into your plan. Call your aunt or your grandmother or a neighbor. Yet another way food brings people together. And sniff! Remember, every bite you have taken in your life is uploaded to your olfactory software. You know what you like, and smelling good is our first clue that we are in for a fine meal. Cooking is about customizing exactly how YOU like things to taste, and what YOUR body is telling you that you need. Seasoning can be done throughout preparing a dish, but taste, always! If you are considering adding an herb, sniff your dish, then sniff the herb. Maybe add a pinch to a spoonful, and see if it is going in a direction you like. Be brave.

Chicken and dumplings is what many Midwestern folks remember from their grandmother's kitchen. Like pot roast, it is primarily a braise, and sets you free for much of the time it is cooking. I feel sure that the old cliché 'tastes like chicken' evolved with the factory raising of meat chickens, butchered around 6-8 weeks. Like people, it takes time for a chicken to develop taste, and there is a definite differences in flavor between the hormone and antibiotic infused infant chickens and one that has run around and chased bugs and made friends for more than a few weeks. The latter our ancestors would recognize, and are worth looking for. They may be called 'roasters' and the larger they are the more favor there usually is. Dark meat has more flavor than light meat 9it is dark because a healthy chicken has walked around and developed some circulation in its legs and thighs, but never flown. To make things easy, especially when you pull the meat off the bone, I use chicken thighs, but a whole chicken works just fine and may be thriftier. Also, make sure the skin and bone are left on for flavor, even though you'll be getting rid of them later.

While Grandmother's chickens were likely carrying salmonella, they also carried the antibodies, or they would be dead. With the advent of factory farming, and (ahem) less than ideal conditions, salmonella became much more of a problem and antibiotics became common. Now we are extremely cautious with raw chicken, as most do carry salmonella, which has now become antibiotic resistant. That said, there is a controversy around washing your chicken. My feeling is this: by washing, you dilute the germs but also spread them more easily. I don't rinse, but rather keep the chicken contained in a large bowl, so it can't touch anything, pat dry with paper towels that go in the trash immediately and the chicken moves from the chicken to the cooking vessel without touching anything. I wash my hands well, vinegar rinse, and don't touch the chicken again.

As for the dumpling recipe, I don't remember anyone in my family making this with anything but 'whomp' biscuits from a tube. The dumpling recipe I use I have had for since I cooked in Alaska in the 70s and was told then that it was over one hundred years old. It was rolled thin and cut with a knife, almost like noodles. I've never found a way to improve it.

Chicken and dumplings, chicken soup and chicken pot pies are kissing cousins. Add stock to the basic recipe and you have soup, maybe with some noodles or rice stirred in. Top with biscuits or wrap in a crust and you have the others. Something to keep in mind. This does take some time and making enough to freeze gives you dinners for the future. My grandmother's freezer as well as my mother's were full, and felt very much like security for survivors of the Great Depression. The one in the 30's.

Chicken and Dumplings
Serves four with leftovers

8 bone in, skin on chicken thighs or

1 whole chicken, cut up or

a combination of pieces

salt and pepper

fat for browning

3 Tablespoons butter

1 cup chopped carrots

½ cup chopped celery

1medium onion, chopped

2 cloves minced garlic

1/3 cup AP flour

5 cups chicken broth

½ can evaporated milk

½ teaspoon dried thyme

½ teaspoon dried sage or 1 teaspoon chopped fresh

¼ cup minced fresh parsley

Pat the chicken pieces with paper towels and season with salt and pepper. (Mix them together in a small bowl so you can use it without contaminating the salt and pepper shakers.) Put a large Dutch oven on the stove over medium heat, and add enough fat to cover the bottom. When it starts to 'shimmer' add enough chicken to cover the bottom with ½" at least between pieces. Cook on both sides until golden brown, and use tongs to remove to a plate. Work in batches, adding oil as needed. When all the pieces are cooked, let cool, and pull off the skin and discard. (How do dog free people cook?)

Add the butter to the chicken fat over medium heat, then add the carrots, onions and celery and cook, stirring, until softened, 7-10 minutes. Add the garlic, cook for one minute or until you smell it cooking. Stir in the flour and scrape to get any browned bits mixed in. When it starts to brown, add the broth, stirring to prevent lumping, the milk and the herbs. Layer the chicken in the pot, drop the heat to medium low, cover and cook for one hour, until tender.

Pull the chicken out and move to a cutting board. Once it cools, remove it from the bone and chop. Discard the bones, skim the fat from the sauce and return the chicken to the pot.

Dumplings
Serves 6

2 cups flour

Almost a teaspoon of baking powder

1 Tablespoon Crisco or lard

2 Tablespoons minced parsley

¼ teaspoon salt

¼ teaspoon pepper

3/4cup warm chicken stock

In a wide bowl, mix the flour, baking powder, parsley, salt and pepper, then use a fork to cut in the fat. Add the stock, using the other hand to work it into the flour mixture, kneading as little as possible. When it starts to come into a ball, cover it with a dish towel and let it rest ten minutes. You may not need all the broth, so add any left into the chicken and sauce.

Rollout on a lightly floured board, cut them as you like (bite size, biscuit size, circles, irregular, with a cookie cutter...) Bring the chicken and sauce to a low simmer and drop the dumplings 2 or 3 at a time into the pot. This keeps them from sticking together. When they are all in, stir gently once, cover and let them simmer for fifteen minutes. Taste and season if necessary. I have been known to run the whole pot under the broiler for a minute or two, no more, just to get a little crust on the dumplings.

Chapter Eight: Smokin'

'A dream starts a dancin' in my head'

Jude Fry

It is difficult to imagine cooking without refrigeration, but that is how much of the world still feeds itself. Salting, fermenting, canning and drying helped us through the millennia, as well as smoking. By the time

Pete came along, the smokehouse, of the kitchen porch was mostly used for storage and as a venue for ghost stories for impressionable grandchildren. But for decades, it served a purpose, and also made for some delicious meals. Jerky benefits from a time over cold smoke, as do many other meats.

When we think of adding smoke flavor now, we either turn to liquid smoke or grilling. But to add enough smoke to preserve the meat without overcooking it, the fire needed to be offset so it was cool before it got to smokehouse. This meant a firebox that could be tended without opening the smokehouse door. Not an elaborate setup, but enough investment that it got a lot of use to justify it.

Perhaps because a pig yielded so much meat, pork is what we commonly think of when we think of smoked meat. Sausage, bacon and ham all got a rest in the smokehouse, and if authenticity appeals, building a cold smoker is easier now than it was a hundred years ago. I have built one of plywood to smoke salmon when I lived in Oregon, and a neighbor reported that I had an outhouse in my backyard. If I had planned ahead, I would have cut a half moon in the door. I AM curious what they thought was causing the smoke.

Granddaddy's smokehouse was perhaps 10' x 10' butthat is a fifty year old memory. Certainly for one ham, a ready made smoker is fine. An old refrigerator is the traditional for a homemade smoker as well and if you are doing much quantity, is something to look in to.

There are two ways to cure a ham. A dry cure involves packing the meat in a salt mix, using curing salt, not just table salt. Any iodized salt will give an off taste to your meat, and the curing salt has other additives that help preserve the meat and keep it from spoiling, including about 6% sodium nitrate, which keeps the color from going grey.. My recipe is 3 cups curing salt (aka pink salt, or Prague powder. I like Anthony's brand) to ¼ cup red pepper flakes and ¼ cup coarsely ground black pepper. A cup of sugar is traditional.

Have your butcher skin a fresh ham. For an 8-10 pound ham you the recipe above should be enough. Clear a space in your refrigerator, probably a full shelf, and enough height to accommodate the ham plus a couple of inches. Put a layer of the mix, ½' deep in the bottom of a roasting pan, and lay the ham in. There are a couple of joints, at the hip and the knee. There is extra liquid there, so with a sharp knife, make a 1"cut down to the bone at each joint, spread with the knife and pack well with the mix to draw out the moisture. Use the rest of the mix to cover the ham, rubbing it in well. Cover with plastic wrap and put in the refrigerator. The temperature must be below 40°. Wait 18 days. Seriously. Two and a half weeks. When the ham is ready to smoke, it will be much firmer- almost like wood, and certainly not with any of the wobbliness of raw meat. If it feels even slightly loose, give it a few more days.

When you are ready to smoke the ham, rinse it thoroughly in cool water, and pat dry. A ten pound ham will take five or six hours of cool smoke to finish. If you like you can stop here, with the cured ham, slice it and freeze or freeze it whole. If you have ever had a 'country ham' you know it is very salty. In the Deep South it is often served very thinly sliced on a hot biscuit. Generally though, you will want to soak it for an hour in a couple of rinses of cool water to remove much of the salt, then fry like bacon. And hang on to the bone for making soup stock for beans.

To smoke a fresh ham, you will use a wet brine. There is a little more labor, but it is somewhat faster. You will need a refrigerator space, and a 'brining bag'. You will also a meat injector, (mine comes from Musco, available with the curing salt and brining bag from Amazon) The wet brine recipe is similar to the dry cure. You use the same curing salt, but it is easy to add herbs and spices as well. The 'honey-baked hams' are done with a wet brine, and always turn out well.

Brine for Smoked Ham
For one 8-10 pound fresh ham

1 ½ cups honey

1 ½ cups <u>non-iodized</u> sea salt

2 Tablespoon each coriander seed, mustard seed, black peppercorns, dill seed, whole allspice

6 bay leaves crushed

1 Tablespoon red pepper flakes

½ cup curing salt (see recipe for dry rub, above)

1 gallon filtered water

Bring the water to a boil, add all of the ingredients, stir to mix and dissolve and let steep and cool. The meat will need to stay submerged, which is why the brining bag is easier, but if you choose not to use it, make sure everything that will come into contact with the meat is sterilized. You will also need a weight to put on the top of the ham to keep it submerged, also sterilized. Put the bag into a deep container (I use a 3 gallon plastic container) Call someone to hold the bag open while you pour the brine, making sure all of the spices go in. Add an additional ½ gallon or so of filtered water. Put the ham in, bone side up, and squeeze as much air out as you can before sealing. Alternatively, weight the meat down with a plate, and a weight, submerging it completely. The ham will brine for a day for each pound of meat, so a ten pound ham will take 5 days. Every two days, take a look at it, and inject the brine deep into the meat using the injector. Do this at several locations, especially the thicker areas where the brine will have difficulty soaking in.

When your ham is finished, take it out and discard the brine. Rinse well in cool water, and place on a rack back in the refrigerator to dry for a day. Freeze or continue on to smoking.

The type of wood used makes a big difference in the finished product. Mesquite didn't begin taking over in Oklahoma until the mid 20th century, so it is likely that either oak or the trimmings from fruit trees was the choice for our pioneers. You will be cold smoking, which means the meat won't be directly over the fire. The temperature needs to stay around 150° around the ham, so a small fire, either in another compartment, or well off to the side of the grill is necessary. A cover is needed also.

Start your fire- do not use charcoal starter or instant light charcoal, as the fire will not get hot enough to burn off the taste. You can start the coals elsewhere and move them to the smoke box, then add small amounts of wood as needed to keep it smoldering . Clean the grill in the smoker and brush with oil. Place the ham on the grill, make sure the smoke is reaching the box, cover and open a beer. In half an hour, take a peek and make sure smoke is still flowing, but little or no flame. Ideally, check the inside of the box and adjust as necessary to keep the temperature within a few degrees of 150°. Allow an hour for two pounds of meat.

Take the ham out of the smoker and let it rest for an hour. If you aren't serving it right away, wrap well in plastic wrap or brown paper and refrigerate for up to a week. It freezes well, too, and I would suggest carving and sealing well in one meal sized portions. And don't waste the bone! All of the trouble is worthwhile for what that bone can do to soup beans.

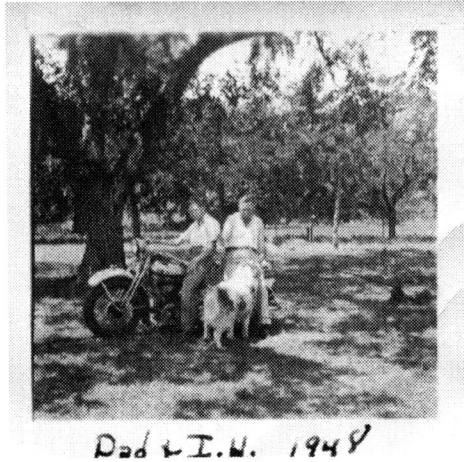

Dad & I.W. 1948

Uncle Pete with his dad and 1941 Harley

Chapter Nine: Food Thoughts

"The corn is as high as an elephants eye

and it looks like its growing clear up to the sky"

For all of us, I think, food connects us and is tied strongly to memories. I would highly recommend that you try writing a food history book for your own family, to preserve the old recipes, add some new ones, but especially to reach out to the folks you have shared the memories with and re-connect. Unlike politics and religion, food discussions around a family gathered to eat rarely end in shouting. And the memories they evoke are always happy.

Another gift the writing of this has given me is a powerful respect, bordering on awe for my forbears and their tenacity to survive in a less than friendly environment. I believe I tend to romanticize those days a lot, probably informed more by visuals of Hop Sing's table on 'Bonanza' than anything resembling reality. It is definitely a first world problem to worry about planning a meal rather than be wondering how to feed a passel of hungry workers with what I have on hand, the grocery store being ten miles away by horse. The difference in work hours between coal and wood heat was huge, as was a wood stove for cooking when it went to propane. Running water in the kitchen, refrigeration, electricity all were such leaps that the invention of the Internet looks a little cute.

Here are some recipes that came out of that culture, based on thrift, and the use of everything edible. Beans, of course. Grandmother's black-eyed peas were a favorite, and we picked and canned them every year, and later picked, blanched and froze them. Use the dried if you must, but if you can find them fresh, it makes a world of difference, especially with immature beans broken into inch long sections and added as 'snaps.' If you do use dried (actually any dried bean) soak overnight in cool water, drain in a colander and rinse a few times during the day. This wakes up the plant inside and gives a livelier flavor as well as better nutrition. When cooking, add a couple of pinches of baking soda, which enhances the creaminess. That and soaking also cut down the cooking time, which was important if you were cutting your own wood.

Home Style Black Eyed Peas

Makes one big pot

6 cups fresh or dried/ soaked black-eyed peas

1 smoked ham bone or hock

¼ cup cider vinegar

2 cups chopped onion

1cup chopped celery

1 Tablespoon minced garlic

1 chipotle pepper, minced, canned in adobo sauce

Fat for frying

2 cups green beans, cleaned and cut in 1" pieces or immature black eyed peas

2 Tablespoons cider vinegar

1Tablespoon honey or brown sugar

Salt and pepper

If you have a crockpot, cover the ham bone with water and the ¼ cup of vinegar let it cook on low overnight. I find a heavy, lidded pot in the oven at its lowest setting works well too. In the morning, pull the bone out, chop any meat and reserve. Heat a skillet with the oil over medium heat and add the onions, celery, garlic and chipotle and cook until well softened. Mix the vegetables into the black eyed peas, add the stock, adding water if needed to cover the peas and cook 20-30 minutes, until tender, skimming as needed. (Dried will take longer.) Add the meat and green beans, cover and cook five more minutes. Stir in the vinegar and honey, taste and season as needed. Drop the heat to very low, until ready to serve.

These are nice cold, tossed with some oil, lime juice and cilantro, a little chopped onion and jalapeno for 'Cowboy Caviar.'

Many of the farmers in Greer County are descended from farmers who immigrated from Germany and Austria. In a dairy based cattle country, veal was common, when the bull calves were slaughtered. Oklahoma and Texas were much more beef ranchers, although Granddaddy did have dairy on the farm in the late 1930's. He and Uncle Pete delivered milk to about 15 customers in glass bottles, and eventually a truck would come pick up the ten gallon cans. But mostly, it was beef cattle, Herefords and Angus. The German settlers missed their schnitzel, but selling the expensive cuts tend leave much resembling their veal cutlets. I am not saying chicken fried steak originated in Greer County but it could have.

If you have a butcher who can 'tenderize' your steaks for you, have him do that. Much of the point is to use the more flavorful but less tender cuts, so if you have a meat mallet, give the steaks a few whacks. You aren't trying to thin them out, just soften them up a little.

There are several styles of chicken fried steak, but most start with round steak, cut ¾" thick and trimmed of fat. A steak the size of your hand is about right and will weigh about 7-8 ounces. Restaurants often deep free them for expediency's sake and double them in flour, making a thick (and cheap) crust. I prefer pan fried and this is how I remember Grandmother fixing them. Years ago, Billie Dixon, a chef friend and I won 2nd place in cooking competition with her recipe.

Chicken Fried Steak with Gravy
Serves four

2 pounds round steak, ½"thick, cut into six individual steaks

1 cup buttermilk

Texas Pete Hot Sauce to taste

Salt and pepper

1 cup flour

2 eggs

1 can evaporated milk

Fat for frying

Coarse ground black pepper

½ teaspoon dried thyme leaves

If you haven't already, tenderize your steaks by pounding a bit with a meat mallet (or a cast iron skillet)to break down some of the fibers. Don't use meat tenderizer, which will break it down too much. Mix the buttermilk and hot sauce, using more hot sauce than you think you need, as this is a marinade and most of it will go down the drain. Ideally, you have a couple of pigs in the barn who would enjoy it. Put the steaks in a pie plate and pour the marinade over. Cover in plastic, refrigerate and for a couple of hours or so.

Put the flour on a plate and season well with the salt and pepper. Mix the egg with a spoonful or so of water in a shallow bowl or pie pan. Take each steak out of the marinade and let drip. Dip in the flour to coat, then the egg wash and back in the flour. Place on a rack so the batter can meld, and repeat until all the steaks are covered. Reserve the flour mixture for the gravy. In a heavy skillet over medium high heat, bring ¼"of fat (traditional would be bacon drippings or lard or even tallow, but again, you are in charge.) to 325° so a pinch of the flour dropped in bubbles. Lay each steak in the skillet, letting it down so it falls away from you, to prevent a spattering burn. Do not crowd the skillet. As each piece is done, set on the washed rack over newspaper to drain. Add more fat as necessary and bring up to heat before adding the next steak.

The skillet now has something like a roux; the browned flour may be enough to thicken the gravy, or you may need to add more. You want roughly equal parts flour and fat. If there are any burned bits, start with fresh fat, and cook, stirring, over medium low heat until the flour is the color of peanut butter. Gradually add the can of evaporated milk, stirring to prevent burning and lumps. Add more black pepper than you think necessary, then plate a steak, potatoes and gravy, green beans on the side perhaps and a sprinkle of fresh thyme over. Have a seat, dine and prepare to be appreciated.

Mashed potatoes are easy, and if you believe that just get a box of instant. Like cooking eggs, it seems simple, but endless variations are possible. I use red skinned potatoes and leave the skins on to mash them. I like lumps and texture so I use a masher but if you want silky smooth, use a ricer.   This also will separate the skins, so you don't need to peel the potatoes to start. Yukon Gold or russet potatoes can be used, and you will get a different texture.

Mama's Mashed Taters

2 pounds well scrubbed potatoes, peeled if you wish

1 Tablespoon salt

1 cup buttermilk

½ stick butter cut in pieces

Ground pepper, white if you don't want it to show

In a large saucepan, put the potatoes (if they are large cut them up in equal sizes) and the salt and cover with cold water. Over medium heat, boil them for 20 minutes, or until the tip of a knife slips in with little resistance. Drain. (If you prefer, you can peel the potatoes now.) Let cool for five minutes.

If you are using a ricer, position it over a bowl, and process the potatoes or if mashing just move the potatoes to a bowl and mash. Heat the buttermilk, and stir the butter pieces into the potatoes, followed by the warmed buttermilk, stirring just to mix. (Too much beating can make them gummy, which is why a food processor or blender doesn't work.) Add enough buttermilk to get the texture you like, which may be less than a cup, particularly if you are using a masher rather than a ricer. Taste and season as needed, serve.

If you want to guild the lily, you might add some of the pimento cheese you made earlier, or roasted garlic, green chilies or horseradish. Use your imagination, these are a blank canvas.

Something with a little zing to cut the richness is in order and green beans are traditional. If you can't get fresh, frozen work fine, especially the fancy 'French Cut' ones. Just don't waste your time with canned ones. Mother made these often and if there were leftovers, they were lovely tossed into a salad. These are not the brilliant green and crunchy green beans we eat now, but rather then almost khaki colored ones that have cooked long and slow. Don't let the color put you off, what they might miss in picture pretty they make up for in flavor.

Mama's Dilly Beans
Serves 4-6

4-5 slices bacon, chopped

¾ cup chopped yellow onion

2 pounds fresh green beans, cleaned and trimmed

½ cup water

2 Tablespoons cider vinegar

2 Tablespoons honey

Salt and pepper

½ teaspoon dill seeds

Ina heavy saucepan cook the bacon with the onions until they are golden brown, then remove to a bowl and reserve. Toss the green beans with the bacon fat in the saucepan, to coat, add the water, dill seeds, vinegar and honey, drop the heat to low and cook until tender, about 30 minutes. Add the onions and bacon back to the pot and simmer another few minutes. Serve, garnished with fresh dill fronds if available.

Finally,Grandmother's Dilly Rolls. These were everyone's favorite, but especially my cousin Kent's. He would be a tough adversary in a Dilly Roll Eating Contest.

Grandmother's Dilly Rolls
Makes 2 dozen

1 cup whole milk

½ cup sugar

1 Tablespoon instant dry yeast

1 cup buttermilk

1 onion, minced

½ cup finely chopped fresh dill or 2 Tablespoons dried

1 Tablespoon dill seed

2 teaspoons salt

Five plus cups all purpose flour

1 stick of butter

Heat the milk until a drop feels warm on the inside of your wrist. Whisk in the sugar and yeast until dissolved, then add the buttermilk, whisk again and let sit until it begins to foam.

In a large bowl, stir the flour, dill, onion, salt and dill seed together to mix. Melt half the butter and stir into the yeast mixture, then slowly stir in to the flour mix to form a sticky dough. Turn out on a floured board and knead for five minutes, until it begins to come together and feel smooth. Grandmother said it should feel like your ear lobe. Wash your bowl, dry and butter it well, add the dough and cover with a clean towel. It will double in size in an hour or so. I find a glass bowl, with a mark or a rubber band stretched around it helps keep track of when it doubles. It is even better if you let it rise slowly in the refrigerator overnight. Punch the dough down, and leave it on the counter to rise again, about an hour.

Turn back out on a floured board, roll out to 3/4" thick, and using a juice glass or biscuit cutter, cut out a piece, roll between your hands to form a ball. When everything is shaped, place 2" apart on two well buttered baking sheets, and brush the tops with the remaining butter, melted. Let rise once more, for about half an hour, then bake at 400° until brown, about 15-20 minutes. Move to a rack to cool.

These freeze well, if you roll them into balls, then freeze on a sheet pan and move to a bag when frozen solid. To use, place on a buttered sheet pan, and let thaw and rise, about 2 ½ hours, depending on the temperature in your kitchen. Then brush with butter and bake according to the recipe.

By doubling the size of the rolls and flattening them, you can make some rather amazing hamburger bubs...

Acknowledgements

Always the tough part, because like most things, writing a book, even a small one like this, does take a village and I hate to forget anyone.

Uncle Pete (I.H. Stimson of Granite) is the most agreeable and patient man I ever met, but I suspect my hounding him the last few months tried that. He is the last member of his generation and was the source for many of the memories.

My cousin, David Brookins, has always been fascinated by history, and while I archive recipes, he has spent several decades (yes, we are that old....) archiving the photographs and documents that comprise our family's history.

Jennie Mae, Bobbie Jean and Frances Lawana, my grandmother, mother and aunt, were all generous enough to share their kitchens with me over the years. Most of what appears here is their work and memories.

And of course my gracious friends who have supported me with this and other books. When I get focused on a project, I am known to babble and Bruce Thompson, Billie Dixon, Nancy O'Neil and Patrick Darnell read galleys at one time or another and did the brutal editing that is impossible to do for oneself. Maria Pacheco and my husband, Don Lewis often picked up slack to give me time to write.

Thanks to everyone else, and I hope this can give you a glimpse into a simpler time.

Elaine DiRico

Austin, Texas

December 2016